THE BASICS — INSTRUCTION MANUAL FOR

LIFE

ON PLANET EARTH

THE BASICS — INSTRUCTION MANUAL FOR

LIFE

ON PLANET EARTH

dream big

**GET REAL. ACHIEVE HAPPINESS.
ESTABLISH SOVEREIGNTY.**

R.J. MORTON

CONTENTS

Why
This Book...

Life is a onetime gift, a miracle.

But there's a catch.

To be successful in life, all people need Basic Training. It is a priceless asset in the process of forging a character of eternal value established in this realm for the one that follows.

After miraculously coming to be through the love of parents, we are ultimately responsible for co-creating our own essence in appearance and action. ...

Is

Needed...

W e live in a magnificent, awe-inspiring universe that was created in Love for all people, each of whom has infinite value, beauty and purpose.

However, it is up to each individual to fulfill his or her own potential within a "reality" bubble in the larger world of humanity. That human world is distinct from nature. What could have been the crowning achievement of a magnificent universe, is not. It is torn by an invisible war of values resulting in crime, disease and conflict. Success and happiness are not givens, and that "reality" bubble is not even real.

What is actual and normal in the human realm is based solely on perceptions. Such "norms" are what friends say or that which is popularized across society or dictated by governments and institutions in the time and particular space of one's early life. Deeper values are instilled after birth by our parents, with love and more by actions than words. However, the co-creator of each human life is "I", independent of time or location.

What happens when you get lost in the wilderness or find yourself trying to survive as a prisoner of war in a foreign land? What had seemed a deep-rooted sense of home and normality is suddenly revealed as arbitrary. Basic training in the military reinforces mind-body unity, discipline, teamwork and a crystal-clear understanding of where one stands right now in not-always-nice surroundings.

Such education is distinct from the conditioning imposed by one's childhood, peer group or generational and regional cultural bubbles. It is much more important than mass media propaganda and a 4-year liberal arts education that currently [2021] attunes one to false and perverse Marxist-Leninist values and can take a lifetime to pay off.

Basic Training means coming to terms with Reality (with a capital R) through daily discipline and discovery. Character is the bedrock for each child's future family and legacy on Earth.

Tough love of children by their parents is just as important as the "quality time" they spend together. Establishing meaningful standards of behavior for them tells children their parents genuinely care for them.

The destination, after all, is Happiness (with a capital H).

...And

Was Written

This book makes no claim to ultimate wisdom or exclusive insights. It's simply a compilation of things people should know if they don't already, fundamental guidelines that can bring the universal quest for happiness within reach.

We live in an infinite universe, and each human being likewise has limitless potential.

Constant awe at that realization prompted this offering to all who might benefit.

Life on Earth is brief. When we leave it behind, the record of our life experiences for better or worse will be etched in the eternal Book of Life.

That said, let the future begin!

– The Author

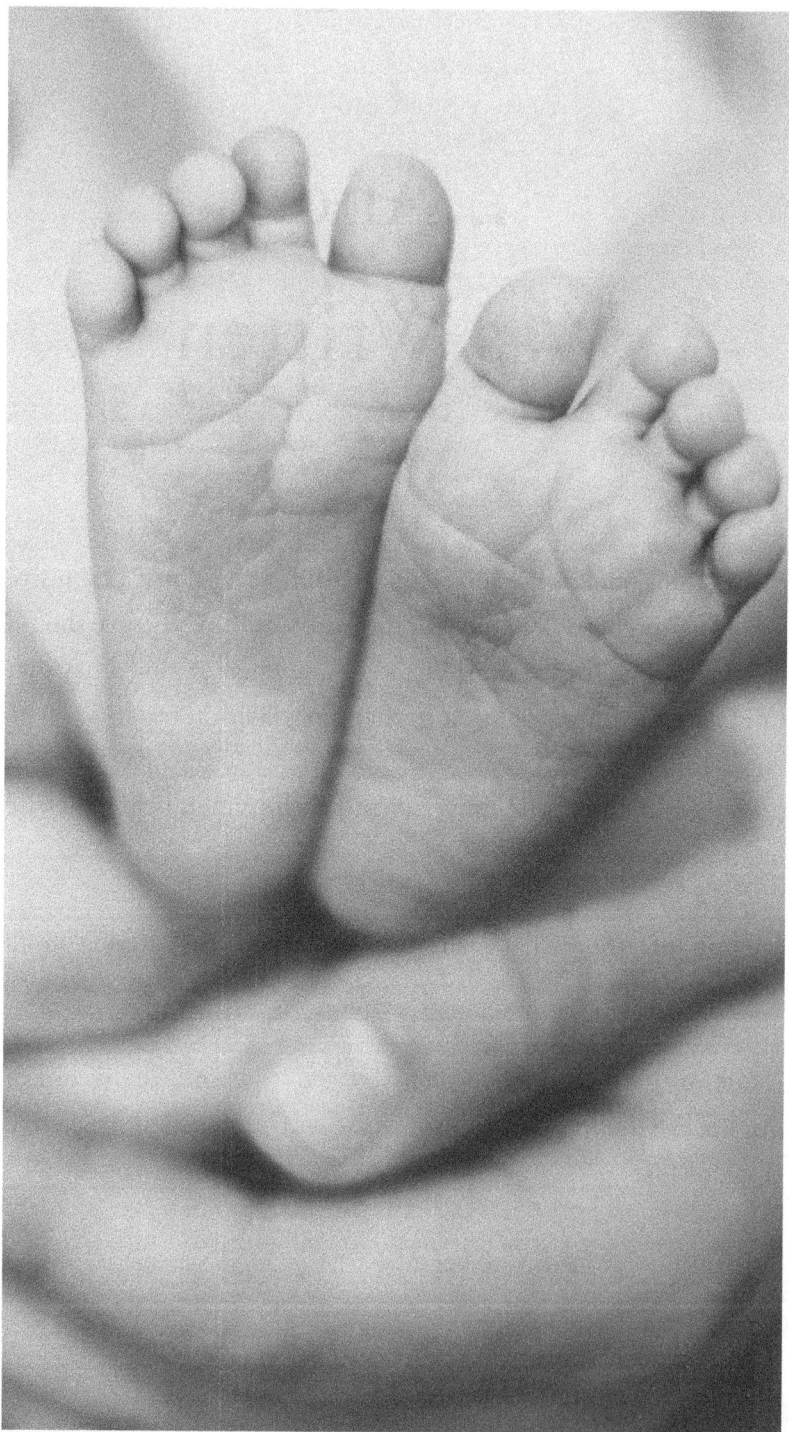

From

Ideal

When Husband and Wife unite in Love, what comes naturally are miraculous children, bright and shiny like new pennies.

These magical bundles arrive without instruction manuals. Their happy parents do research, consult doctors, go shopping and draw on lessons from their own upbringing and generation.

As babies grow from adorable infants into their more rambunctious early years, parents begin to train them, setting limits and establishing consequences for their actions.

To
Reality...

Soon enough it becomes evident that the child's will and that of its parents are not identical. And then comes the multi-dimensional environment outside the loving home which is much more than childhood friends and teachers. Although it's not fashionable to say in secular society, some of those human influences are good and others are evil.

Recall the fictional Tarzan, the awesome savage, who grew to adulthood in nature with no human influence.

What came on Earth as a pure and perfect child with the spark of life many believe to be Divine must grow in a field of humanity that has been corrupted by an evil we would rather not contemplate. That culture is controlled by the invisible enemy of the Creator of Love and poses an existential threat to every child's fundamental happiness, health and very life.

It's a stealth dimension we cannot avoid. It manifests in unexpected ways in our minds and emotions and relationships. It can even

impact physically through disease, crime, war or other misfortune.

Parents naturally shelter and shield their children from all harm but as they grow, they must find their way in this world and learn by experience.

As children become independent, they must navigate through constantly-changing and unpredictable circumstances. They see about them a world of natural beauty but where man-made evil lurks, always presenting as desirable and wonderful like the forbidden fruit in the Biblical Garden of Eden.

There are drugs and diet and lifestyle options that drain one's energy and potential. But there are even more destructive influences which can lead to catastrophe.

Consider the shocking 2020 documentary "ContralLand" [produced by: https://www.vets4childrescue.org/] about the widespread and expanding pedophilia networks pervasive on the "dark web" of the Internet. They involve established members of society [the documentary includes footage of members of the U.S. Government who were detained] as well as the "scum of the earth". These networks target children of all races, classes and nationalities. It is slavery of the most horrific and perverse kind that traces back to the beginning of human history.

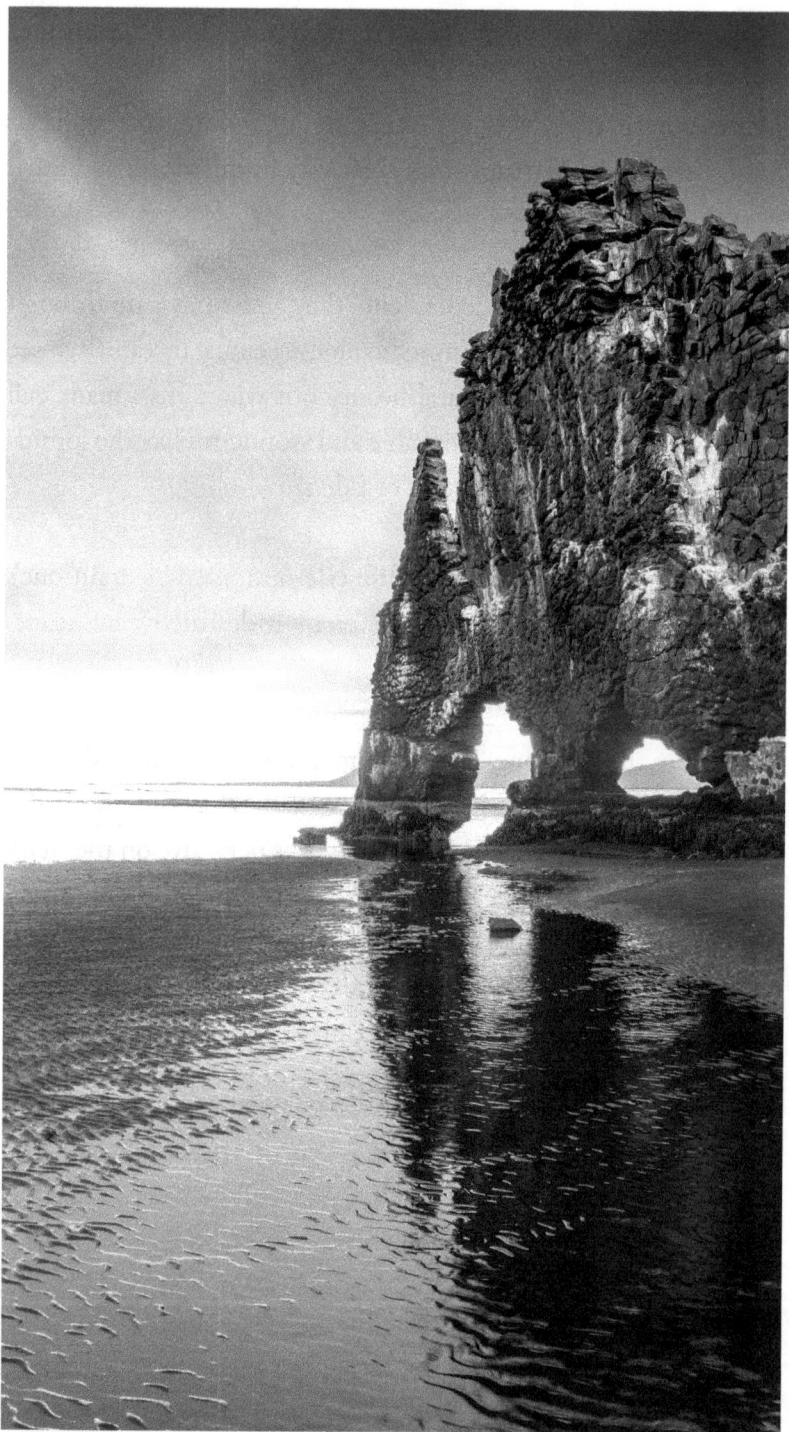

...And Fulfillment

God, the loving Heavenly Father of the Judeo-Christian tradition and the origin of all cultural spheres, did not create this evil environment which breaks and tortures His heart continuously, according to the Korean teacher Sun Myung Moon (1920-2012). The Bible most accurately and centrally records God's continuous effort to restore His lost children after the "Fall" when humanity was expelled from the Garden of Eden (Genesis 3) or the realm of the original ideal.

In the Biblical account, His "Salvation Providence" proceeded through Noah and the flood judgement followed by the establishment of a family, tribes and nation (Abraham, Isaac, Jacob, Joseph, Moses). This included the remarkable reconciliation between Jacob and Esau which served to heal the tragic precedent for humanity of the disunity between Cain and Abel. All of this history, presented in lurid detail in the Biblical record, was the prelude for the coming (and the Second Coming) of the Messiah.

Through the "Words of Life" in the Holy Bible and in the New Truth that followed, parents can find the secrets to raise their children to be happy, healthy, successful and victorious in life on Earth.

This manual is certainly no substitute for other forms of necessary education. It is offered for all who realize that the infinite beauty of a newborn infant was not meant to be temporary but, on the contrary, should characterize the entirety of its life on Earth.

Get Real, Achieve Happiness, Establish Sovereignty

"*As a result of the Fall, human beings fell into spiritual ignorance. This meant humanity was fundamentally ignorant regarding God's existence, the meaning of life, and the entire universe. Accordingly, people did not know how they should live their earthly lives, that there is a spirit world after death, and that the former should properly prepare them for the latter.*"

– Sun Myung Moon on his 80th birthday (2000)

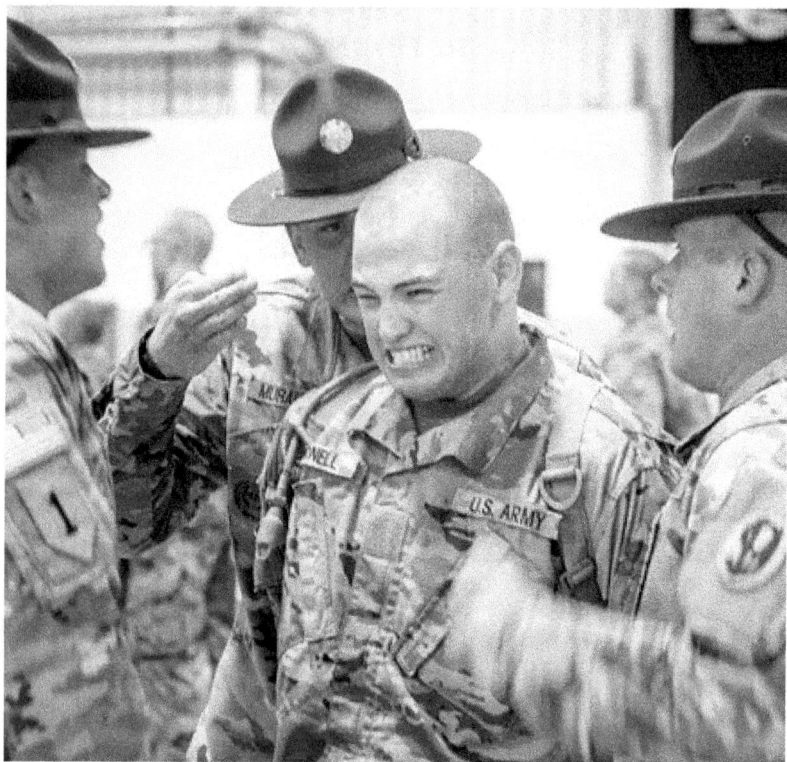

Vulnerability

Like their Creator, all are created in His likeness (*"Male and female created He them."*— *Genesis 5:2*) and are bequeathed Freedom and Responsibility. Then they are destined to procreate with the same Divine Love.

But first comes the learning curve.

And because there is unnatural evil that enjoys sovereignty in this world, all people and even their Creator are vulnerable to setbacks, attacks, pain and suffering.

Even the perfect Creator? If He has the Heart of Parents, He must be just as vulnerable if not more so than His children.

The Bible and human history offer dramatic records of adversity on the long road to restoring the happy original state in the Biblical Garden of Eden.

The happy conclusion lies ahead, the inevitable destination. We, like God, can restore our lost but destined sovereignty on Earth through unity, training and action in Love.

In the process of growing to adulthood, each and every person must learn wisdom and discernment to distinguish between natural good and unnatural evil.

Devastation in the Ghouta suburb of Damascus, Syria in early 2018. / WorldTribune.com

Myself and Everyone Else

"T oday you should not strive to satisfy your own desires, but rather must lead lives of faith and sacrifice in serving a higher purpose. Then you should attain the standard of the heart of Jesus who went through hardships for God's will and for humankind."

– Sun Myung Moon

What set apart the great Biblical figures Noah, Abraham, Jacob, Joseph, Moses and Jesus?

What is unique about these Providential men is that they all left behind their own comforts and self-interests in response to God's call and the wellbeing of their future generations.

That standard of sacrifice for a higher purpose once resonated powerfully in the popular culture of great Christian civilizations including the United States of America. It is the ticket to lasting happiness.

True Freedom

We are created with Free Will. Our free actions can bring life or death, happiness or misery, heaven or hell, prosperity or abject poverty.

Actions in quest of temporary joys do not bring lasting happiness and can even cause premature death. So, wisdom, discipline and sound education are necessary in this world.

There are no guaranteed do-overs in real life.

Free Will actions in ignorance can have tragic consequences.

We must train ourselves well and not deprive those whom we love of the Words of Life.

What are the Words of Life?

They are the words that come directly from God about which more will be said later. They are the seeds of True Love, the keys that unlock our original Divine nature.

The fruit of these seeds are free actions that bring lasting happiness.

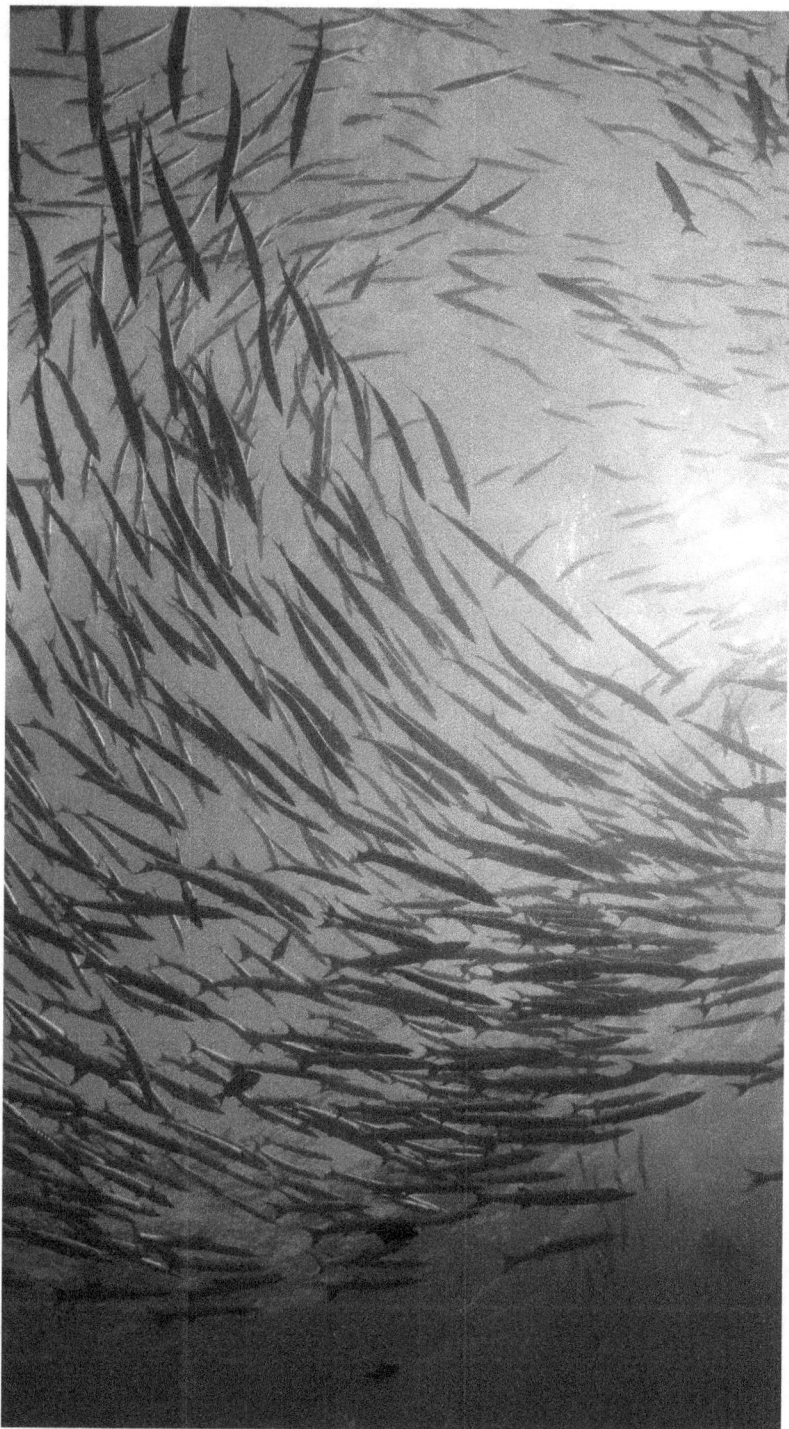

Purpose

For life to have meaning, it must have purpose. It's not complicated.

Each baby is instilled with a spark of Divinity. So, he or she is intended to grow over about 21 years into maturity or oneness with the Creator* [Matthew 5:48], marry a spouse who had done the same and have a family that shares an intimate bond with God.

Each person is also born with unique gifts and qualities allowing him or her to render special service to their bloodline and community which was intended to be intimately inclusive of God.

By searching for and praying to know his or her unique purpose, and acting in response, each person can find fulfillment in life.

* *"Be perfect, therefore, as your heavenly Father is perfect."*
  – Matthew 5:48

Sovereignty

When our original mind is in charge of our bodies, and the selfless love of God guides our relationships and actions, then the proper order in the universe is the result.

Glimpses of this ecstatic joy at the core of all being inspires us to work for the world of Love and eternal happiness.

When our original ancestors' happiness and purpose were not achieved in the Garden of Eden as recorded in the Bible, a disastrous human history resulted.

By following the Words of Life, princes and princesses can prevail in a hostile environment and become Kings and Queens prepared to reign over the creation as originally intended.

So God created man in his own image, in the image of God created He him; male and female created he them. And God blessed them, and God said unto them, Be fruitful, and multiply, and replenish the earth, and subdue it: and have dominion over the fish of the sea, and over the fowl of the air, and over every living thing that moveth upon the earth. — Genesis 1:27-28

Physical and Spiritual Nourishment

13 TRACKS OF DISCIPLINE AND DISCOVERY

TRACK ONE

Enjoy a **healthy diet of both physical and spiritual food**. One eats 3 meals a day. What you eat is important to sustain your physical integrity, strength and energy. Eat plenty of vegetables and adequate protein. Eat carbohydrates as needed for physical exertion. Limit carbohydrates if you start to gain too much weight. Each person should become closely attuned to what his or her body really needs in terms of nourishment to be energetic, healthy and active in carrying out their minds' commands.

But in the words of Jesus,
"Man does not live by bread alone."

Exercise:

- What did you eat today? Did you pay attention to what you chose to eat?

- Did you eat more or less than you needed to accomplish your activities?

- Did you have a balanced diet of nutritious food?

- How will you eat differently tomorrow?

Optimal Nourishment

TRACK TWO

O
ur instincts impel our physical selves to search out and eat food. Feeding the spirit self is more important because it lives on after physical death. But it stems from a more subtle impulse and involves the Free Will.

If one's spirit is not growing daily, deterioration sets in which impacts the physical body and mind and causes unhappiness. A quiet time to consume and digest 'Words of Life" at the start of every day is essential for mental, spiritual, emotional health and happiness. Prime examples of the Words of Life are the Holy Bible [https://www.biblegateway.com/ for one] and Cheon Seong Gyeong [http://www.unification.net/csg/CheonSeongGyeong. pdf].* At the end of each day, one should reflect and privately report to God and conscience about that day's actions with gratitude and perhaps repentance.

"Our spirit man grows through the give and take action between the 'life element' (positive) coming from God, and the 'vitality element' (negative) coming from the physical man."[1] The vitality element' is defined as follows in which man refers to both men and women:

[T]he physical man provides a certain element to the spirit man, which we call the "vitality element". In our everyday life, we know that our mind rejoices when our body performs a good deed but feels anxiety after evil conduct. This is because the vitality element, which can be good or evil according to the deed of man, is infused into our spirit man.

The Divine Principle, written by Sun Myung Moon in the closing days of the Korean War, also teaches that the spirit grows through

1 Divine Principle, Part I, Chapter I, Section VI, 3. THE RECIPROCAL RELA-TIONSHIP BETWEEN THE PHYSICAL MAN AND THE SPIRIT MAN. https://christkingdomgospel.org/divine-principle/part-1-chapter-1-principle-creation/#

three stages of growth like the physical body. But unlike with one's body, that growth is not automatic but requires discipline and positive actions in line with the Words of Life.

When one's spirit is growing daily, one feels energetic and happy, and one's physical body is most likely to be healthy.

Exercise:

- What spiritual food did you consume today?

- If you did not read World of Life, did you consume some form of entertainment by reading or video?

- What positive actions did you take today?

- What spiritual food will you consume to start the day tomorrow?

*See Appendix for more information on "Words of Life"

The Fundamental Spiritual Laws

TRACK THREE

Memorize the **Ten Commandments,** the fundamental spiritual laws that gave birth to Christianity and modern civilization. While intended for the "Chosen People" of Israel, they apply to all religious traditions.[2] They are our Creator's loving guideline for life in this world He made for us. Nazism, Communism, and ISIS revealed the barbaric realms that result when these principles are erased. <u>See below</u>:

– Exodus 20: 1-17

And God spoke all these words: "I am the Lord your God, who brought you out of Egypt, out of the land of slavery.

1. **"You shall have no other gods before[a] me.**

2. **"You shall not make for yourself an image in the form of**

---

2 Israel's purpose was to receive the Messiah whose mission was to reunite all religions and peoples.

anything in heaven above or on the earth beneath or in
the waters below. 5 You shall not bow down to them or
worship them; for I, the Lord your God, am a jealous God,
punishing the children for the sin of the parents to the third
and fourth generation of those who hate me, 6 but showing
love to a thousand generations of those who love me and keep
my commandments.

3. "You shall not misuse the name of the Lord your God, for
the Lord will not hold anyone guiltless who misuses his name.

4. "Remember the Sabbath day by keeping it holy. 9 Six days
you shall labor and do all your work, 10 but the seventh day
is a sabbath to the Lord your God. On it you shall not do any
work, neither you, nor your son or daughter, nor your male or
female servant, nor your animals, nor any foreigner residing
in your towns. 11 For in six days the Lord made the heavens
and the earth, the sea, and all that is in them, but he rested on
the seventh day. Therefore, the Lord blessed the Sabbath day
and made it holy.

5. "Honor your father and your mother, so that you may live
long in the land the Lord your God is giving you.

6. "You shall not murder.

7. "You shall not commit adultery.

8. "You shall not steal.

9. "You shall not give false testimony against your neighbor.

10. "**You shall not covet** your neighbor's house. You shall not covet your neighbor's wife, or his male or female servant, his ox or donkey, or **anything that belongs to your neighbor.**"

Exercise:

- Memorize and practice both speaking and writing the Ten Commandments.

- For each commandment, translate it into modern language and reflect upon its meaning in your daily life.

The Core Motto for Life on Earth

TRACK FOUR

The **Two Great Commandments** as taught by Jesus. [Matt. 22:36-40] This with the Ten Commandments form the skeleton of an ethical life that fosters stability, health, prosperity and positive karma/fortune for future generations.

Jesus said unto him, Thou shalt love the Lord thy God with all thy heart, and with all thy soul, and with all thy mind. This is the first and great commandment. And the second is like unto it, Thou shalt love thy neighbour as thyself. On these two commandments hang all the law and the prophets.

– Matthew 22: 36-40

"Teacher, which is the greatest commandment in the Law?"

Jesus replied:

1 "**Love the Lord your God with all your heart and with all your soul and with all your mind.**'[a] 38 This is the first and greatest commandment. And the second is like it:

2 '**Love your neighbor as yourself.**'[b] 40 All the Law and the Prophets hang on these two commandments."

Exercise:

- Memorize and practice both speaking and writing the Two Great Commandments

- For each commandment, translate into modern language and reflect upon its meaning in your daily life.

Jesus said unto him, Thou shalt love the Lord thy God with all thy heart, and with all thy soul, and with all thy mind. This is the first and great commandment. And the second is like unto it, Thou shalt love thy neighbour as thyself. On these two commandments hang all the law and the prophets. MATTHEW 22:37-40 (KJV)

Know: You were intended to be God's child

TRACK FIVE

Act accordingly. God is not self-centered. The fallen world of Satan is totally self-centered.

True humanity implies responsibility for others that stems from the recognition that all humans were meant to be your brothers and sisters. Such unity can only occur in a God-centered world.

Recognize and uphold the Divine value and pure, selfless and fearless character in others. Do not acknowledge and reinforce in others the opposite traits inherited from the Human Fall and which are still dominant in our human environment.

Exercise:

- Think about three people you interact with on a day-to-day basis. How do you conduct those relationships in terms of the above?

- How do you view those three people?

Dream Big

TRACK SIX

You have limitless potential for greatness and happiness that stems from your Divine origin. The nature of God and His realm of cause is to actualize what your original mind deeply desires and directs through your conscience even if it involves performing seemingly humble tasks. That is unique to each person, and fulfillment is within reach in countries not shackled by tyrannical governments.

Exercise:

- What would you love beyond all else to accomplish during your life?

- How would the fulfillment of that dream benefit humanity?

Teach children all the Bible stories

TRACK SEVEN

I f God indeed exists, where else can one find the most central chronicle of His involvement with fallen humanity and the battle between good and evil culminating in the first advent of Christ on earth? Like the movie 'Groundhogs Day', these themes continue to repeat in modern life and are the foundation of education. One thing that is deceptively evil about secular society is its constant pressure to erase the moral foundations of Western, Christian civilization. Take away the common law and the definition of right and wrong, good and evil and one is left with a barbaric, communistic society such as was glimpsed in the rampaging mob rule in June 2020 in the United States and in the "no-go zones" in several western European nations.

Exercise:

- What story from the Bible has made the most lasting impression on you?

- Review the Bible or your favorite selection of Bible stories for children and select one you could share with your child or those with whom you are close.

Enjoy a healthy, active lifestyle.

TRACK EIGHT

Avoid sugar drinks and take only small portions of fast food. Embrace physical exertion in work and play. The universe works on the principle of Give and Take in terms of energy and love. The more one gives, the more one receives.

Exercise:

- Look at yourself in the mirror first thing in the morning. Do you look like someone who leads a healthy, active lifestyle?

- Is physical work or vigorous exercise in your schedule today?

- If your answer to either of the above is 'No,' make a list of realistic lifestyle changes you can enthusiastically embrace.

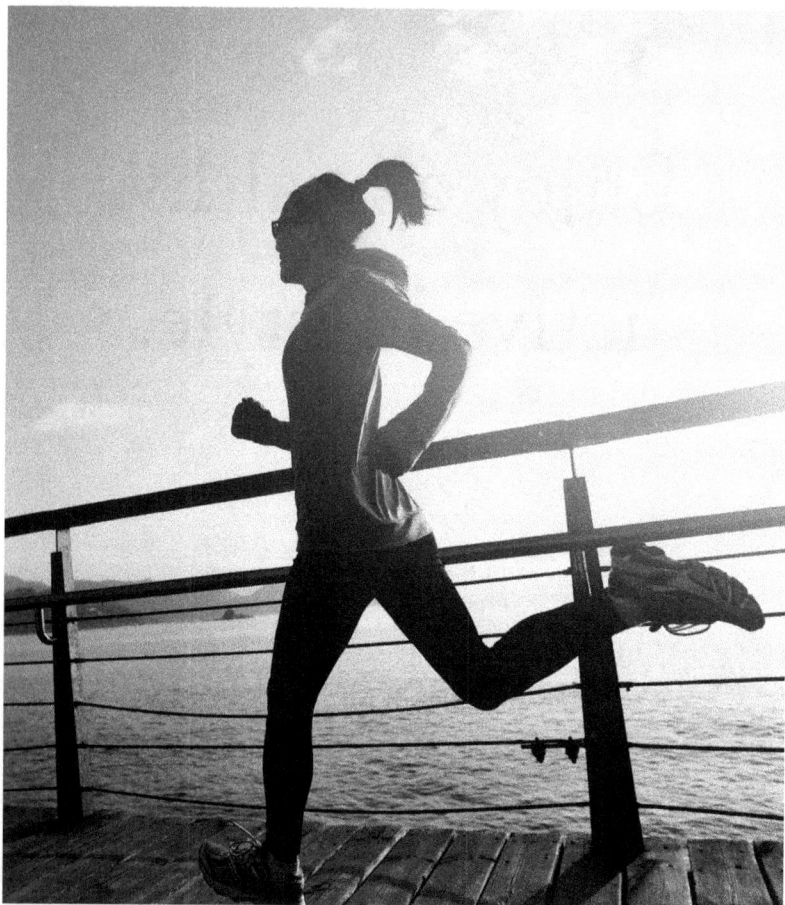

Look your best at all times

TRACK NINE

Be modest but attractive in dress, appearance and manner. Look your best at all times. You are after all the unique child and representative of God. Like God, you should aspire to live for the sake of others. You can best do so by inspiring others to be like you and to please and bring joy to your direct family members and your Creator.

Exercise:

- Look at yourself in the mirror in the morning after washing, grooming and dressing yourself for the day ahead. Do you like what you see? Would your spouse or your family members like what they saw?

- Check your smile. Is it crooked? Do some practice!

- How about your clothing? Is it time to donate some items, try others you haven't been wearing or plan to go shopping?

Be humble, not boastful.

TRACK TEN

God, the invisible and all-powerful Creator is everywhere, and we are always in His presence. Those who know or believe this will behave accordingly. The human ego, which draws sharp distinctions between yourself and your surroundings, is essential for survival. But the ego should always be subordinate to the mind and conscience. The very life and death of Jesus Christ, even more than his words, testify to the selfless and limitless giving which is Divine Love. Humility is the outward manifestation of this quality but does not imply meekness or self-negation. Whether believers in God or not, happy and productive people have an inner peace that is the opposite of self-worship.

Exercise:

- Take inventory of yesterday's thoughts and actions, excluding work or education. Were they self-centered, service-oriented or something else?

- Ask yourself the same questions about your plans for tomorrow.

- Take a look at your life as a whole in terms of motivation and aspirations. Be honest with yourself. Most people want to be successful in work and school and to have a happy family. What are your life goals and why?

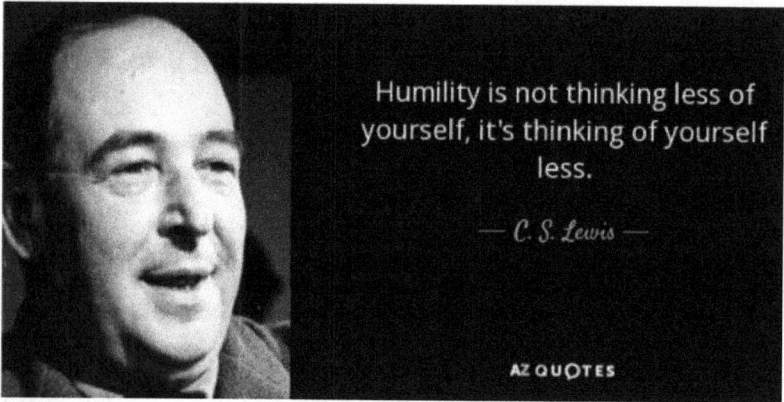

Humility is not thinking less of yourself, it's thinking of yourself less.

— C. S. Lewis —

AZ QUOTES

Divine Purity is Majestic

TRACK ELEVEN

All forms of sexual expression are strictly reserved for the eternal marriage bond and one's marriage partner, not self. Such is the key to understanding what went wrong in the Garden of Eden. The unity in pair systems through love and energy is a fundamental principle of the universe. The integrity of a truly victorious human being springs from this simple fact.

Exercise:

- Think about the above in relationship with the training you have been subjected to by the popular culture.

- Think about the above in relationship with the training you have been subjected to in "Family Life Education" or "Sex Education" or similar classes in public education.

- If the above is true, how does it apply to your behavior?

Champion True Normal

TRACK TWELVE

The Fall from God's Ideal of True Love came from the selfish misuse of love and free will which became false love and the false normal. Therefore, the assumptions or "norms" in our surroundings must be evaluated objectively rather than taken at face value and assimilated. "Champion" means to invest your full heart with energy and spirit.

Exercise:

- Consider your peer community. Would they consider you strange if you spoke positively about your parents, for example, or about your nation or God?

- How would you contemplate changing the norms of your peer group?

Champion
True Natural

TRACK THIRTEEN

Living primarily according to self-centered motivations, rather than for God and others, is unnatural. The opposite is the ultimate and destined norm that brings ultimate Happiness. "Champion" means to invest your full heart with energy and spirit.

Exercise:

- Where is your life headed and why?

- Evaluate your list of things to accomplish today according to the above criteria.

- Did your evaluation of your to-do list cause you to make changes? What were they?

Spiritual Slavery

D ue to the Fall recorded in the first book of the Bible [Genesis 3], people's minds and bodies came under the dominion of Satan's false love, which in turn made them into egocentric, and consequently, dysfunctional individuals. The resulting families, societies, nations and world were not what God intended in the Garden of Eden. This is hell on Earth and the reason that the Lord's Prayer says: "Your Kingdom come, your will be done, on Earth as it is in Heaven."

Jesus said:

> 44 You are of your father the devil, and your will is to do your father's desires. He was a murderer from the beginning, and does not stand in the truth, because there is no truth in him. When he lies, he speaks out of his own character, for he is a liar and the father of lies.
> - John 8:44 English Standard Version (ESV)

An especially sobering view of the reality of evil is the documentary

ContraLand about the stealthy pervasiveness of pedophilia in modern society and the irreversible damage it does to its young victims.

Words of Life hold the keys to overcoming evil on the personal level.

> Do not be overcome by evil, but overcome evil with good.
> – Romans 12:21

The New Testament Gospels of Jesus explained the role of the Messiah in reversing the Fall of Adam and paving the way for humanity to return to its original intended state of oneness with God and having nothing to do with evil.

> [16] For God so loved the world that he gave his one and only Son, that whoever believes in him shall not perish but have eternal life.
> - John 3:16 New International Version (NIV)

Jesus taught that such salvation involved Free Will and required total transformation.

> [6] Jesus answered, "I am the way and the truth and the life. No one comes to the Father except through me.
> - John 14:6 New International Version (NIV)

> [3] Jesus answered him, "Truly, truly, I say to you, unless one is born again[b] he cannot see the kingdom of God."
> - John 3:1-21 English Standard Version (ESV)

Christians have understood this to mean a "born again experience" where one is baptized and feels like a "new creature in Christ. However, Paul lamented that he could not overcome sin.

> [15] I do not understand what I do. For what I want to do I do not do, but what I hate I do. [16] And if I do what I do not want to do, I agree that the law is good. [17] As it is, it is no longer I myself who do it, but it is sin living in me. [18] For I know that good itself does not dwell in me, that is, in my sinful nature.[a] For I have the desire to do what is good, but I cannot carry it out. [19] For I do not do the good I want to do, but the evil I do not want to do — this I keep on doing. [20] Now if I do what I do not want to do, it is no longer I who do it, but it is sin living in me that does it.
>
> - Romans 7:15-20 New International Version (NIV)

The Divine Principle of Sun Myung Moon explains this paradox. Christ came to fulfill God's simple formula for life on earth and happiness: **The family.**

Jesus as the second Adam was to have had a family from which would spring a new lineage connected directly to God and free from Satan's bloodline. All of his followers who lived by this template could do the same over time. Because Jesus's life and ministry were cut short, the "Second Coming" was to complete his mission.

To be "born again" is to eliminate evil, not only in the eternal world but here on earth through one's family.

Trailblazers

We look to our parents and memorable teachers and leaders for examples, focusing on their strengths. In the Biblical record, Noah, Abraham, Jacob, Moses, Jesus have withstood the test of time and merit review regardless of the arbitrary and temporal dictates of conventional wisdom:

There is no other way to set up a standard for ourselves but by observing and studying all of the central figures in God's providence from Adam on. Let us look at Noah, Abraham, Moses, John the Baptist, and other dispensational figures. We must be curious about their objectives and motives. This will be the issue.

All of these great men started their life of faith centered not on themselves, but on God. Why do we have to respect them? Simply because they were guided by God, not by themselves. Also, we should know what kind of life they lived for God in their age. We find that they all had a conflict — their life of faith versus the life of reality. We find further that they were not of one will when they faced these conflicts, but that they solved the problem when they brought themselves to center on God, not on their own desires. And we know that because of this conflict between God's side and the world's side, these people endured persecution and suffering. That is why they are great people. ...

For years Noah could only think of building the ark and went to the mountain to work there. Do you think there is a woman who can endure ten years with such a husband? An American wife sues for a divorce if her husband goes away for six months. Noah's work was not an ordinary task. Therefore, this event must have been the greatest event after God created man. And if a wife starts to persecute her husband, the children will also do the same with her.

How much pain Noah must have felt in his heart when his family could not understand him? Because of this he had great troubles. When he asked his family to get him something to eat, or something to wear, they treated him as if he were a beggar. Noah could stand the persecutions outside of his family — from the village or from the nation. But these sufferings and persecutions were coming from inside his own family, the most difficult for him to bear. In spite of that, he had to finish his work. He had great confidence, great faith in God. Noah's life was full of persecution and rejection — he was entirely alone. But he couldn't cast off God, though he had to forget all others. His wife and children might have felt sometimes that they would have liked to kill him. But the more he received persecution from his environment, the more whole his heart for God became. He became separated from his circumstances and his community. He became separated from the world, so he came into the position where he could receive God's love. If he had rejected those people who persecuted him, then God's will wouldn't have been fulfilled. But Noah sacrificed himself for those who persecuted him. Instead of causing them to suffer, Noah had a mind to forgive their sins for God. He was standing in the position of the unfallen brother asking God to forgive the fallen brother and sister and willingly bearing all the difficulties. Noah had such a heart. Because of that heart God could proceed in His providence of restoration. The position of complete self-denial centered on God — that was Noah's position.

This same principle can be applied elsewhere — for example, in the cases of Moses and John the Baptist.

Moses went the same course. He spent his youth in the Pharaoh's palace. But when he saw his people suffering, he left the Pharaoh's palace. He killed an Egyptian who persecuted Israelites. Moses' position was to save Israel, in spite of the danger. But the people of Israel didn't receive Moses, who tried to save them. They persecuted him and expelled him to the wilderness of Midian. There for 40 years Moses longed for God, loved God, and made a resolution to save his people. Because of that intention, God chose him to free the Israel people from Egypt.

—*"Faith and Reality" (Twelve Talks of Sun Myung Moon), 1970-1973.*

Freedom and Responsibility

As people grow and mature into their adolescence, they become responsible for their actions springing from their Free Will. This is the most exhilarating time of life for all men and women but also the most consequential and fearful.

From then onward, each person owns his or her own record that is engraved in the eternal Book of Life.

'That said, the story begins ...'

Appendix I

Words of Life

People are born with a physical body, which lives 70 to 100 years or so, and a spiritual body that lives on for eternity.

Both need quality nourishment on a regular basis to enjoy good health and happiness. Physical food becomes irrelevant after leaving this life. Spiritual food helps form the thoughts and actions in this life that shapes the eternal character.

In this book, "Words of Life" refer to enlightenment and truth that comes directly from God or through those with whom He has achieved oneness. Lives guided by Words of Life can return people to their originally intended relationship with the Creator of Life.

The words of Jesus are recorded in the four Gospels in the Bible: Matthew, Mark, Luke and John[3].

Sun Myung Moon said that in prayer at the age of 16 in North Korea (1936), Jesus appeared to him and asked him to complete his mission on Earth.

After years of research and prayer he began to teach and preach the Gospel in South Korea and later in newly communist North Korea where he was imprisoned in a concentration camp. After being liberated by invading U.S.-led UN forces following the Incheon Landing, he walked on foot to Busan, South Korea where

---

3 Holy Bible, New Testament. The first four books are Matthew, Mark, Luke and John. https://www.biblica.com/bible/niv/matthew/1/

he published "Divine Principle"[4]. Before his death in 2012, he published in 2006 a volume called "Cheon Seong Gyeong"[5] comprised of thematically selected segments from his thousands of speeches and sermons. He directed that not a word of it should be altered and offered it for daily reading and study by everyone, regardless of their faith or lack thereof.

4 Divine Principle, Parts I and I. https://christkingdomgospel.org/archives/divine-principle/

5 Cheon Seong Gyeong, Sun Myung Moon, June 13, 2006, (2,543 pages). https://www.sanctuary-pa.org/textbooks

Appendix II

Excerpts from 'Rules for Life: An Antidote to Chaos' by Jordan B Peterson –

Just a few years ago, I was an unknown professor writing academic books that nobody read. Then, with God's help, I decided to stop feeling sorry for myself and develop my potential.

Pinkos and wishy-washy liberals had cornered the market in cod psychology, so I guessed there must be a huge hunger for a self-help book, backed up with religion, mythology, CAPITAL LETTERS and stating the obvious – one directed at responsible, socially minded conservatives craving some pseudointellectual ideology to prop up their beliefs. And bingo! Here are my Rules for Life.

1. **Stand up straight with your shoulders straight.** There is a God who wants us to have Order. Order is Masculine and Chaos is Feminine. Therefore, to move towards Order, we all need to man up.

2. **Treat yourself like someone you are responsible for helping.** The story of the Garden of Eden shows that we are all touched with Original Sin But you have a choice. You can either seek Heaven or be dragged down into Hell. Yes, you have a shameful, sinful nature but for God's sake just make a bit of an effort.

3. **Befriend people who want the best for you.** Some people are beyond help. They are merely exploiting the willingness of good people to help them and, as Dostoyevsky rightly

observes, will drag you down to their level. So stick with the winners.

4. **Compare yourself to who you were yesterday, not the useless person you are today**. Start by getting on your knees to pray. Even if you don't Believe in God. Atheists are merely people who are blinded to the true way of Being.

5. **Do not let your children do anything that makes you dislike them**. Remember that children are born with Original Sin and have a huge capacity for Evil. They are not Innocent Beings. They need Discipline if they are going to grow up to be even vaguely worthwhile humans. And slap them if necessary – don't listen to what the lefties say.

6. **Set your house in order before you criticize the world**. Remember the story of Cain and Abel? Well, read it then. Yes, Abel was a schmuck who deserved to die, and Cain wasn't quite as goddamn perfect as he thought he was. He deserved to die, too. We all deserve to die. So, stop moaning if someone is richer and better looking than you.

7. **Pursue what is meaningful, not what is expedient.** Quit looking for short cuts.

8. **Tell the truth. Or at least don't lie**

9. **Assume the person you are listening to knows something you don't**. Just shut up, quit moaning and listen.

10. **Be precise in your speech.** Confront the chaos of Being.

Appendix III

Author's Mottos

- Just because you're paranoid doesn't mean they're not out to get you.[6]

- Don't sit in judgement of anyone above you in the hierarchies. Those individuals have the overview you lack.

---

6 ∞ Based on the Author's years spent working in Washington, D.C.

About the Author

R J Morton owns a company in northern Virginia and has lived there and in Texas, New York, Japan, Tennessee and North Carolina. His early career exposed him to European, Middle Eastern and East Asian cultures. His marriage and family have happily further expanded life experiences. Professional and academic achievements are irrelevant in the larger scheme of things, he says. "You come into this incredible world all alone without even a backpack, and you leave in the same way."

SOURCES

INTRODUCTION: WHY THIS BOOK

1. Page 6: Royalty-free stock illustration ID: 511385842 Shutterstock. Earth Day, small planet in the space, 3d illustration. By Photobank gallery.

2. Page 8: Royalty-free stock photo ID: 1400732387 Shutterstock. Landscape of Mount Huangshan (Yellow Mountains). UNESCO World Heritage Site. Located in Huangshan, Anhui, China. By aphotostory.

PART 1: THE BASICS

3. Page 12: Royalty-free stock photo ID: 670911229 Shutterstock. Newborn. By Yani Kas.

4. Page 14: Royalty-free stock photo ID: 162953912 Shutterstock. Conceptual sign with words reality check ahead caution warning over dark blue sky. By RedDaxLuma.

5. Page 16: Royalty-free stock photo ID: 94224787 Shutterstock. Expulsion of Adam and Eve from paradise. 1) Le Sainte Bible: Traduction nouvelle selon la Vulgate par Mm. J.-J. Bourasse et P. Janvier. Tours: Alfred Mame et Fils. 2) 1866 3) France 4) Gustave Doré. By ruskpp.

6. Page 18: Royalty-free stock photo ID: 779114575 Shutterstock. Huge basalt stack Hvitserkur on the eastern shore of the Vatnsnes peninsula. Colorful summer sunrise in northwest Iceland, Europe. Beauty of nature concept background. By Andrew Mayovskyy.

7. Page 20: Abraham_Willemsens_-_The_reconciliation_of_Jacob_and_Esau.jpg (620 × 466 pixels, file size: 113 KB, MIME type: image/jpeg). https://commons.wikimedia.org/wiki/File:Abraham_Willemsens_-_The_reconciliation_of_Jacob_and_Esau.jpg.

BASIC TRAINING:

8. Page 22: Army recruit being trained in basic training. Date: 31 December 2017. Source https://www.dvidshub.net/image/4060400/welcome-fort-leonard-wood. Author: Stephen Standifird. https://commons.wikimedia.org/wiki/File:Recruit_being_trained.

9. Page 24: Devastation in the Ghouta suburb of Damascus, Syria in early 2018. / WorldTribune.com.

10. Page 26: Royalty-free stock photo ID: 1937399083 Shutterstock. Sunset on blue sky. Blue sky with some clouds. Blue sky clouds, summer skies, cloudy blue sky. By OlegRi.

11. Page 28: Royalty-free stock photo ID: 519883603 Shutterstock. School barracuda fish and scuba divers. By Rich Carey.

12. Page 30: Parents with child Statue, Hrobákova street, Petržalka, Bratislava, Slovakia. Date: 14 July 2006. Source: Own work. Author: Kelovy. https://commons.wikimedia.org/wiki/File:Parents_with_child_Statue_Hrobakova_street_Bratislava.JPG.

13. Page 32: Royalty-free stock photo ID: 1341069152. Healthy organic food on dark background. Vegan and vegetarian diet food concept. Clean eating. Top view, flat lay. By Tatjana Baibakova.

GUIDELINES FOR DAILY LIFE:

14. Page 34: Royalty-free stock vector ID: 1840845973 Shutterstock. Collection of vitamin B12 food. Cottage cheese, eggs, sea food, fish, meat, dairy product. Dietetic products, organic natural nutrition. Flat vector cartoon illustration isolated on white background. By GoodStudio.

15. Page 36: Sermon on the Mount by Carl Bloch (1877): Dansk: Bjergprædiken, Object type painting Edit this at Wikidata, Genre   religious art Edit this at Wikidata, Date: 1877. Wikimedia Commons, the free media repository. Medium: oil on copper. https://commons.wikimedia.org/wiki/File:Bloch-SermonOnTheMount.jpg.

16. Page 38: Royalty-free stock photo ID: 1714301218 Shutterstock. Monk Holding Bible Looking Up to God Sky Light, Old Priest in Black Robe in Storm Mountains. By Inara Prusakova.

17. Page 41: The Ten Commandments, Official Trailer, Paramount Movies, Video Image

18. Page 42: Royalty-free stock photo ID: 328480373 Shutterstock. God is love concept text lying on the rustic wooden background. By ChristianChan.

19. Page 48: Royalty-free stock photo ID: 161016020 Shutterstock. Portrait of a young aviator parked aircraft. By Vasilyev Alexandr.

20. Page 50: Royalty-free stock photo ID: 447689434 Shutterstock. Milan, Italy. Cathedral made of Candoglia marble. David and Goliath - biblical story. By Tupungato.

21. Page 52: Royalty-free stock photo ID: 255001651 Shutterstock. Healthy lifestyle sports woman running on wooden boardwalk sunrise seaside. By lzf.

22. Page 53: Old 1940s sepia photo of dreamy young woman looking in theater mirror. Royalty-free stock photo ID: 673467163 Shutterstock .By Ysbrand Cosijn.

23. Page 56: Azquotes.com https://www.azquotes.com/quote/174171. www.azquotes.com/picture-quotes/quote-humility-is-not-thinking-less-of-yourself-it-s-thinking-of-yourself-less-c-s-lewis-17-41-71. Humility is not thinking less of yourself, it's thinking of yourself less. - C. S. Lewis.

24. Page 58: Royalty-free stock photo ID: 146933723 Shutterstock. Young couple kissing outdoor in summer sun light. Kiss love date color evening teen. By solominviktor.

25. Page 60: Royalty-free stock photo ID: 1347105503 Shutterstock. People helping each other hike up a mountain at sunrise. Giving a helping hand, and active fit lifestyle concept. Asia couple hiking help each other. By peampath2812.

26. Page 62: Royalty-free stock photo ID: 134407094 Shutterstock. Happy woman jumps to the sky in the yellow meadow at the sunset. By My Good Images.

27. Page 66: The Temptation of Christ. Wikimedia Commons, the free media repository. Object type: painting. Date: 1854. Medium: painting

28. Page 70: Royalty-free stock photo ID: 135555482 Shutterstock. Couple Lovers walking on the beach. By ndphoto.